Robotics:
FROM AUTOMATONS TO THE ROOMBA

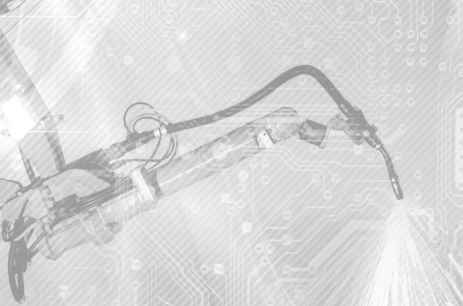

Essential Library

An Imprint of Abdo Publishing | www.abdopublishing.com

History of Science

Robotics:
FROM AUTOMATONS TO THE ROOMBA

by Racquel Foran

Content Consultant

Lisa Nocks, PhD
Senior Lecturer
NJ Institute of Technology

ASIMO

History *of*
Science

www.abdopublishing.com

Published by Abdo Publishing, a division of ABDO, PO Box 398166, Minneapolis, Minnesota 55439. Copyright © 2015 by Abdo Consulting Group, Inc. International copyrights reserved in all countries. No part of this book may be reproduced in any form without written permission from the publisher. Essential Library™ is a trademark and logo of Abdo Publishing.

Printed in the United States of America, North Mankato, Minnesota

102014
012015

THIS BOOK CONTAINS RECYCLED MATERIALS

Cover Photos: Denis Klimov/Shutterstock Images; Pavel Isupov/Shutterstock Images; Shutterstock Images
Interior Photos: Denis Klimov/Shutterstock Images, 1, 3; Pavel Isupov/Shutterstock Images, 1, 3; Shutterstock Images, 1, 3, 13, 14, 34; Shawn Baldwin/AP Images 7; Brian Snyder/Reuters/Corbis, 9; Reuters/Tokyo Electric Power Co/Corbis, 10; Stefano Bianchetti/Corbis, 17; Thanassis Stavrakis/AP Images, 18; Matt Rourke/AP Images, 23; Bettmann/Corbis, 25, 29, 31; BBC/Corbis, 27; Geoff Caddick/Press Association/AP Images, 33; Eddie Worth/AP Images, 37; Ralph Crane/The LIFE Picture Collection/Getty Images, 39; Matt Dunham/AP Images, 41; Peter Menzel/Science Source, 43; SSPL/Getty Images, 44; Rainer Plendl/Shutterstock Images, 47; Uli Deck/picture-alliance/dpa/AP Images, 48; Charles Knoblock/AP Images, 51; Y. J. Ishizaki/AP Images, 52; Vasily Smirnov/Shutterstock Images, 55; NASA, 57, 59; US Navy, 62, 81; Robson Fernandjes/picture-alliance/dpa/AP Images, 65; Rick Friedman/Corbis, 67; Itsuo Inouye/AP Images, 69; Susana Bates/Sipa USA/AP Images, 70; Rich Pedroncelli/AP Images, 72; US Air Force, 75, 77; US Army, 79; US Marine Corps, 85; Koji Sasahara/AP Images, 87, 95; Jacquelyn Martin/AP Images, 88; Eric Risberg/AP Images, 93

Editor: Arnold Ringstad
Series Designer: Craig Hinton

Library of Congress Control Number: 2014943875

Cataloging-in-Publication Data
Foran, Racquel.
 Robotics: from automatons to the Roomba / Racquel Foran.
  p. cm. -- (History of science)
 ISBN 978-1-62403-564-7 (lib. bdg.)
 Includes bibliographical references and index.
 1. Robotics--History--Juvenile literature.   I. Title.
 629.8--dc23

                                                     2014943875

Contents

Robot
RESPONDERS

$$\frac{a+b}{a} = \frac{a}{b} = 1{,}618$$

It was September 11, 2001, in the heart of New York City. Fires raged at unbearable temperatures. Dust and smoke filled the air, impeding both sight and breathing. The stability of the structures in the area was unknown. It looked like a scene from a disaster movie, but it was terribly real. After being hit with hijacked jetliners, the 110-floor twin towers of the World Trade Center had crumbled to the streets of Manhattan. People ran toward the catastrophe in an effort to save lives. However, emergency responders were blocked by rubble in their search for survivors. Piles of debris could have collapsed without warning.

Robots were brought to the scene to assist in the rescue effort. One type of robot used was the PackBot. These tough little robots, looking like two miniature tank treads topped off with crane arms, could get into places emergency workers could

The rubble of the World Trade Center created an extremely hazardous environment for human responders.

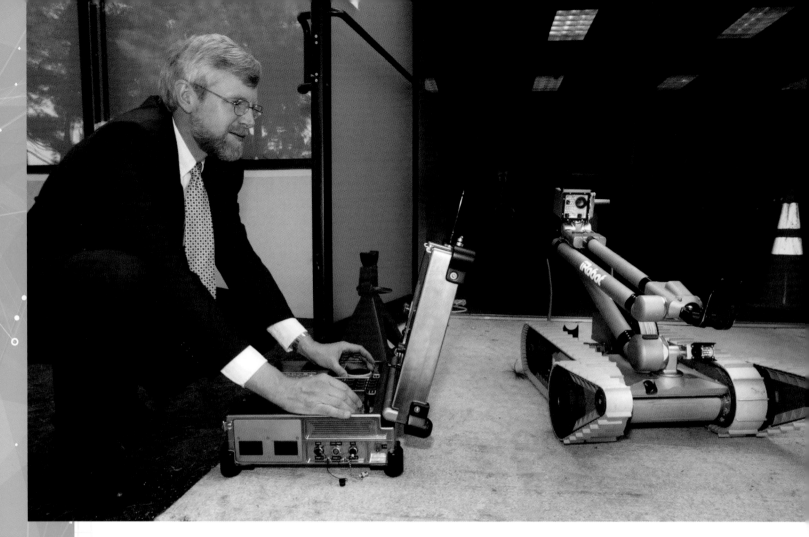

The remote-controlled PackBot can navigate difficult terrain on its tanklike treads.

not. Working in tight, poorly lit spaces with little or no oxygen, these hardy machines could get into nooks and crannies to look for survivors and assess the stability of the debris.

No survivors were found by robots at the World Trade Center site, but it is likely PackBots did save lives. By testing the structural stability of buildings around the disaster area, they were able to prevent workers from entering potentially dangerous areas. The robots that were used were still under development. According to Joe Dyer of iRobot, the company behind PackBot, the robots were "literally pulled out of the laboratory and taken to 9/11."[1] The disaster led to increased spending on rescue robots. The US government dramatically increased funding for its military robot programs. It focused on researching and developing robotic vehicles of all kinds.

Emergency Robots in Action

The attacks of September 11 had not been the first disasters to demonstrate the need for these robots, but they were a major example of how such robots could help. Within ten years, robots had advanced enormously. Their use in war zones, disasters areas, and other emergency situations became commonplace.

Robots were a natural response to the Fukushima Daiichi Nuclear Power Plant disaster in Japan. In March 2011, an

ROBOT TASK FORCE

While the disaster at the World Trade Center was unfolding on the morning of September 11, 2001, one man took the lead in getting a diverse team of robots deployed to the site. Lieutenant Colonel John Blitch served his last day with the US Army on September 10. When he heard the news about the attacks on Manhattan, he put on his uniform and headed for New York City. Blitch had spent three years leading a military robot program. The program had funded several academic and corporate research efforts to make robots that could replace human soldiers in dangerous situations. Within six hours of the attacks, Blitch and other robot teams were at the site. In total, 17 different models of robots were used on the disaster site over an 11-day period.[2]

earthquake shook the region, and a tsunami hit the coast hard. It left the nuclear power plant damaged and leaking radioactive material. The radiation was so hazardous it was impossible for any human workers to approach the plant to assess the severity of the damage. Once again, the PackBots were there to do the job. Equipped with video cameras to provide live images, as well as temperature sensors, the robots entered the reactors to observe damage, map the radiation levels, and assist with the cleanup. An unmanned helicopter took aerial photos of the plant. Three years later, robots were still working at the site in places where humans could not.

From Fiction to Reality

Assisting humans in dangerous situations is one of the most common practical uses of robots. However, PackBots and robots like them do not resemble the humanlike machines that usually come to mind when thinking of robots. Robots are used for hundreds of purposes all over the world, but very few look like the humanoid robots depicted in science fiction. This has been a common theme in the history

Authorities sent multiple PackBots into the radiation-saturated nuclear power plant.

PACKBOT

The PackBot was built by the robotics company iRobot, best known for its Roomba robotic vacuum cleaners. The robot development began in the 1990s with the financial support of the Defense Advanced Research Projects Agency (DARPA). This US government agency funds high-tech projects that have military applications. Since first developing the PackBot, iRobot has shipped more than 3,500 customized units to military and police forces worldwide. In addition to the work the PackBots did at disaster sites in New York City and Japan, they have also been used for observing enemy combatants and disposing bombs in Afghanistan and Iraq. The PackBot was inducted into Carnegie Mellon University's Robot Hall of Fame in 2012.

of robotics. Reality is always trying to catch up to the expectations fantasy creates.

Advances in robotics have frequently been driven by the imagination of fiction writers. A science-fiction playwright coined the word *robot* in 1921. The word *robotics* came from a later science-fiction story. The books, television shows, movies, and video games that have informed our view of robots have also challenged those working in the field of robotics to make science fiction into science fact. In return, as scientists develop more and more advanced robots, science-fiction writers have been forced to be more creative in order to keep their fiction a step ahead of fact.

The Field of Robotics

Robotics, established in the mid-1900s, is a relatively new field of science. It brings together several disciplines, including mechanical engineering, electrical engineering, and computer science. All robots are made up of three main components: a device that interacts with its surroundings to accomplish tasks, sensors that collect information about

DEFINING *ROBOT*

The word *robot* was first used by Czech playwright Karel Čapek in his 1921 play *R.U.R. (Rossum's Universal Robots)*. In what would become a common science-fiction theme, the play is about robots created by humans to serve them. The robots eventually take over and threaten to destroy the human race. The word *robot* originates from the Czech word *robota*, meaning forced labor or drudgery. In his 1941 short story "Liar," American science-fiction writer Isaac Asimov gave the science of robots a name: robotics. Robotics is the engineering discipline dealing with the design, construction, and operation of robots.

Today's advanced robots would have seemed like science fiction only a few decades ago.

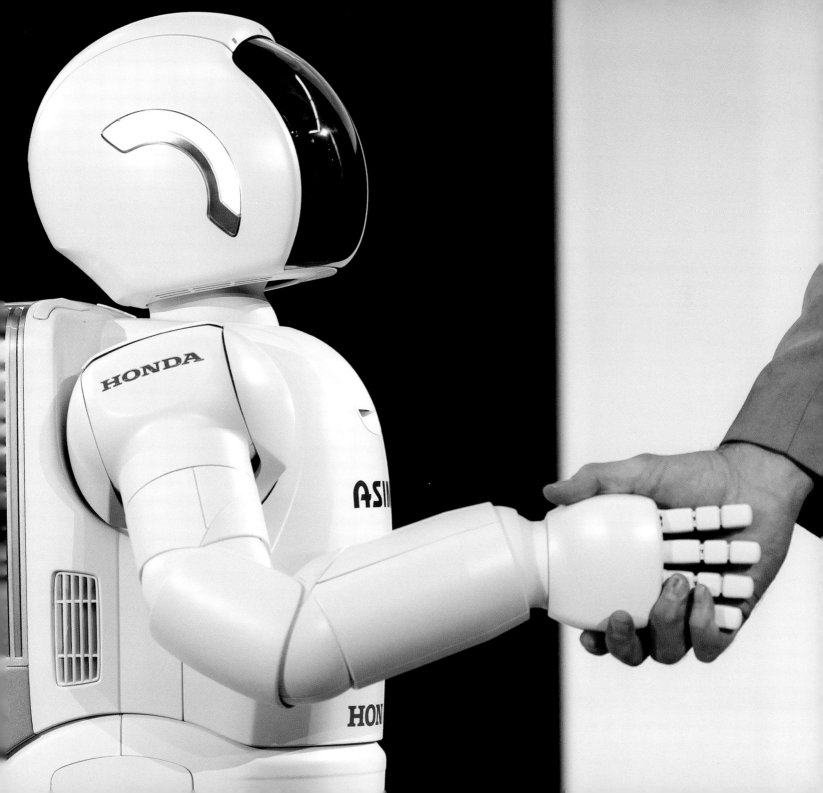

their environment, and a system for the device and sensors to communicate with each other.

It was not until after the first industrial robots were put into use in the early 1960s that research and development of robotics began to accelerate. Technology had finally begun catching up to the dreams of science-fiction authors. The field of robotics has been growing by leaps and bounds ever since.

Today, domestic robots such as the Roomba vacuum are found in thousands of households. Industrial robots assemble cars and other complex machines in factories. Robots assist soldiers, surgeons, and other professionals. Some help scientists explore deep space and the depths of the ocean. The technology behind all of these robots has only become possible in the last few decades. Yet the earliest ancestors of today's robots date back thousands of years.

Robotic vacuums are now a common sight in homes across the world.

ROBOTS IN THE MOVIES

Robots have been capturing audience imaginations on movie screens since the 1920s. The robot Maria from the 1927 silent movie *Metropolis* was the first of many robot movie stars. In 1939, moviegoers were introduced to Iron Man, a remote-controlled robot invented by his operator to "crush all opposition."[3] The 1951 film *The Day the Earth Stood Still* introduced audiences to the tall, metallic Gort. Perhaps the most popular movie robots of all time are R2-D2 and C-3PO from the Star Wars series of films. Robocop, the Terminator, and the Transformers are among the best-known robots in today's films.

Early AUTOMATONS

$$\frac{a+b}{a} = \frac{a}{b} = 1.618$$

Long before the word *robot* was introduced in science fiction, humans imagined machines that could do the work of people. The ancient Greeks built devices called automatons for amusement and theatrical purposes. An automaton is a machine capable of reproducing a preset sequence of movements under its own power. The first of these devices was a wooden pigeon made in approximately 380 BCE by Archytas of Tarentum. The pigeon was attached to a bar on a pivot that moved in a circular motion using compressed air.

Perhaps the most practical of the ancient automatons was the clepsydra. A clepsydra is a water clock. It uses the consistent flow of water to raise a float. The float holds a pointer that marks the passage of time as it rises. The clepsydra is believed to have been first invented by the ancient Babylonians in approximately 1500 BCE, but

The water clock was among the earliest devices to reproduce a predetermined set of mechanical movements.

Only fragments of the Antikythera mechanism remain intact.

its basic design was improved upon over the centuries. In approximately 270 BCE, the Greek physicist and inventor Ctesibius created a very accurate water clock. Its dial took a full solar year to make a complete revolution.

There is evidence the Greeks developed other sophisticated mechanical devices. In 1900, a diver discovered a shipwreck off the coast of the island of Antikythera. The wreck was a cargo ship from approximately 150 BCE. It contained what is now known as the Antikythera mechanism. At first, the discovery did not seem like much, but when examination of the heavy bronze mass revealed 30 gear wheels of various sizes, researchers realized the significance of their find. It is the most complex geared mechanism known to have come from ancient times. Initially, its purpose puzzled researchers, but they now believe the device is a mechanical calendar used to predict astronomical cycles. One part predicted lunar and solar eclipses, another synchronized lunar months and solar years, and a large gear in the middle indicated the position of the moon. The Antikythera mechanism is the oldest ancestor of the clockwork mechanics used in early modern robots.

Moving Machines

Ancient writings indicate there was a strong interest in automatons. In the first century CE, Greek inventor Heron of Alexandria wrote many books that preserved and built on the mathematical and engineering knowledge of ancient times. One of his writings on mechanics, the *Pneumatica*, describes a long list of automated devices, including singing birds, puppets, coin-operated machines, and temple doors that opened when a fire was lit on an altar. A work entitled

CLOCKWORK MECHANISMS

Before people learned to harness the power of electricity, many automatons relied on clockwork mechanisms. A clockwork mechanism is a completely mechanical device made up of four main components: a key, a spring, gears, and a mechanism that moves. Winding the key on a clockwork device tightens the spring, which in turn stores potential energy. Releasing the energy sets the gears in motion, and the gears provide motion to the mechanism. Some clockwork mechanisms also have cams or cranks. A cam or crank transforms the motion of the spring to a back and forth motion. In a robot's case, wheels drive the cranks that power the robot's legs. One leg crank is connected to the top of one wheel, while the other is connected to the bottom of the other wheel. As the wheels turn, the cranks rotate out of sync, making the robot take steps. Today's windup toys still operate using this simple clockwork principle.

Mechanica includes writings on the theories of motion and balance as well as ways to lift and move heavy objects using mechanical devices. It is not clear how many of these automated devices were actually built by Greek inventors, but the Antikythera mechanism proved they had the precise engineering knowledge needed to build the ones Heron described and many more.

For the next 1,500 years, automatons of all shapes and sizes became more common in countries around the globe. Chinese writings from the 600s to 900s CE describe automatons such as flying birds and an otter that could catch a fish. Muslim engineer and inventor al-Jazari designed some of the most refined automatons of the Middle Ages. His water clocks are described as having included trumpet-playing musicians, birds that opened their beaks, and doors that opened to reveal people. As chief engineer to Sultan Nacer ed-Din Muhammed ibn Qura, he was also required to write a book about engineering. He wrote his *Book of Knowledge of Ingenious Mechanical Devices* in 1206. The illustrations and instructions in the book are so detailed and accurate modern engineers have been able to recreate al-Jazari's designs.

The Europeans also experimented with automatons. Throughout the 1300s and 1400s, automatons were created for the amusement of royalty. Leonardo da Vinci's notebooks of the 1490s reveal blueprints for several automated machines, including a self-propelled cart, a robot knight, and an animated lion. All were designed for the purpose of entertainment. The cart was to be used in theater performances, the robot knight to entertain crowds at a pageant, and the lion to be a gift for King Louis XII. Around the same time, German scholar Johann Müller is reported to have created an artificial flying eagle.

The first documented android, or robot in human form, was created by Hans Bullman in the early 1500s. His androids entertained crowds by playing musical instruments. Automated, lifelike devices were also a common feature on the palace grounds of the wealthy.

It is the 1700s, however, that are considered the golden age of automata. Clockwork mechanics had advanced, and machines were now driven by complex systems of gears and cylinders containing thousands of control tracks, or cams. These tracks were made up of rods of different heights attached to a cylinder. The cams on the cylinder pushed on levers that moved the rods, which in turn moved the automaton in a predetermined series of actions.

The automatons of this era came in all shapes and sizes and varied in complexity of design. They ranged from pocket watches that displayed intricate miniature scenes to full-size

SAINT-GERMAIN-EN-LAYE

One of the most elaborate automated gardens of the 1500s was the royal residence at Saint-Germain-en-Laye. Built in 1598 by Florentine architect Tommaso Francini, the main feature of the garden was a giant water fountain. The Seine River provided water to the fountain. The water flowed into pools on various levels of the garden below the fountain. Tubes ran from these pools to supply other fountains and give power to automatons throughout the garden. It was an impressive display that included several themed grottoes featuring mythological characters. In the Roman god Neptune's grotto, stepping on a hidden tile on the ground would bring the god forward with his trident in hand. Enter another grotto and the Greek hero Perseus came down from the sky to battle a dragon.

THE TURK

Wolfgang von Kempelen built an automaton called the Turk in 1770. It toured Europe and the Americas, captivating audiences with its apparent ability to play chess. By the time the Turk was built, people had become used to seeing automated devices. The ability of automatons to move on their own was entertaining, but people understood they were not thinking beings. The Turk amazed observers because it appeared to have the ability to think. It played chess against humans and often won. Many famous people of the time played against the Turk, including French leader Napoléon I and American author Edgar Allan Poe. The workings of the Turk were such a popular mystery that several books were written about the device, including one by Poe. It turned out, however, that it was all an elaborate hoax. The cabinet of the machine was just large enough to fit a skilled human chess player inside. This hidden person operated the machinery that made the Turk move.

androids capable of drawing, playing the harpsichord, and holding a quill and writing text. The automatons were not created for practical purposes. Instead, they were entertainment for the wealthy, adorning the parlors of the upper class. The demands of the French weaving industry would finally start to drive the development of practical automated machines.

Weaving New Technology

In the early 1700s, French weavers struggled to recreate the fine silk outfits with intricate embroidered patterns made by Chinese weavers. The detailed patterns required a large number of threads with needles attached. Weaver Basile Bouchon decided to try applying technology to the weaving loom. His idea was to use perforated strips of cardboard to guide the needles. The concept was very simple: where there was a hole in the cardboard, the needle would go through it and then also go through the cloth. If there was no hole in the cardboard, the needle would be driven back. The process was developed in 1729. It was then improved by Jacques de Vaucanson in 1745.

Some automata were capable of carrying out complex actions, including writing.

Several decades later, Joseph Marie Jacquard hit upon a new idea. He would make the punch cards separate from the loom, allowing them to be swapped out so a single loom could create an unlimited number of patterns. The Jacquard weaving loom was introduced in 1801. It was the first machine to automatically process information. Its punch card system is the earliest ancestor of computer programming systems. It was a critical first step toward allowing computers and robots to operate independently.

VAUCANSON'S DUCK

In addition to automating the weaving loom, Jacques de Vaucanson also invented one of the most complicated and admired automatons of his time. Vaucanson's duck mimicked a live duck. It moved around and adjusted its wings. More amazingly, it ate food, appeared to digest it, and excreted waste. However, this was an illusion. The food was gathered in one container inside the duck, and the waste was stored and expelled from a separate container. The duck required thousands of moving parts in both its body and base to achieve automation. Vaucanson took the duck on tour in 1738. People paid to sit in the audience and watch the duck in action.

The Jacquard loom's punch cards, *top*, made it possible to quickly and automatically reproduce woven patterns.

Chapter
Three

Robots of the
EARLY 1900s

$$\frac{a+b}{a} = \frac{a}{b} = 1.618$$

In the first half of the 1900s, the idea of thinking machines began entering the public consciousness. The word *robot* was first used in the 1921 play *R.U.R.* to describe manmade machines built to look like and be used by humans. Once these humanoid machines had a name, science fiction novels and movies that featured robots became more popular. In 1926, the movie *Metropolis* featured the most lifelike robot to date, Maria. Her metal robot shell set the standard for all future robots. What fiction imagined, inventors tried to achieve.

Robot Invasion

In 1920, inventor A. J. Roberts was seen walking his robot named Kaiser through the streets of the West End of London, in the United Kingdom. The robot moved around on wheels. It was not long before robot sightings like this began happening

The play *R.U.R.* introduced the term *robot* to the public's vocabulary.

at exhibitions and fairs in many countries. In 1927, the electronics manufacturing company Westinghouse introduced the Televox to the world.

The Televox was a device originally sold by Westinghouse to perform basic tasks. It was able to answer a telephone and then perform a few simple functions by operating switches. One of its uses was to monitor water containers in high-rise buildings and turn pumps on and off as needed. At the time, wireless control was not reliable, and installing a new system of wires was impractical and expensive. The Televox overcame these challenges by using telephone wires that were already in place to receive its transmissions. The Televox's practical applications made it one of the earliest modern robotic devices not used for entertainment purposes. When an employee at Westinghouse added a cardboard head, body, arms, and legs to Televox, Westinghouse had its first of many humanoid robots.

WESTINGHOUSE ROBOT MASCOTS

The Televox was just the first of many robots Westinghouse built over the years. In 1932, the more advanced Willie Vocalite was introduced. Willie could sit, stand, salute, and fire a gun. Using voice recordings, it could also speak with a limited vocabulary, and eventually it gained the ability to sing. Willie was demonstrated throughout the United States, drawing crowds wherever it went. In preparation for the 1939 World's Fair in New York City, Westinghouse developed an even more advanced robot. Elektro the Moto-Man welcomed guests to the Westinghouse building at the fair. At seven feet (2 m) tall and 280 pounds (130 kg), Elektro was an imposing figure.[1] It was also talented. It could walk and move its head, arms, and fingers. It also had a vocabulary of 77 words, and it could count on its fingers.[2] Elektro was a huge attraction at the World's Fair and drew a lot of media attention. Before the fair had ended, Elektro had been called "The World's Most Famous Robot."[3] The fair was so popular it was reopened for a second year. For the second year's exhibition, Westinghouse gave Elektro a companion, Sparko the dog robot. Sparko could do tricks similar to those performed by live dogs, but crowds particularly enjoyed watching it obey Elektro's commands.

In 1929, New York City mayor James Walker used a Televox to remotely open a new hospital.

Tesla's Remote Control

In order for scientists to be able to build the robots of people's imaginations, other inventions had to be developed. As the 1800s were coming to an end, Serbian-American inventor Nikola Tesla applied for a patent for a "Method of and Apparatus for Controlling Mechanism of Moving Vessels or Vehicles," more commonly known as a radio or remote control.[4]

Tesla demonstrated his invention using a remote-controlled boat at the 1898 Electrical Exhibition at Madison Square Garden in New York City. People were amazed that Tesla could operate the boat and easily change the direction it was moving while standing many feet away from it. Prior to his demonstration, the patent office had been reluctant to issue a patent, but they were quick to do so once they saw Tesla's boat in motion.

Tesla believed governments would be interested in his new technology for warfare, but there was little interest from militaries or private investors. Tesla's patent expired before remote control ever found use in a serious or practical application. Despite being overlooked at the time, Tesla's radio-controlled boat is ultimately the ancestor to the vast number of remotely controlled robots and vehicles developed over the next hundred years.

Tesla conducted many experiments in electrical and radio technology.

The 1928 London Model Engineering Exhibition opened with a greeting from Eric the Robot. The creation of W. H. Richards, Eric was able to stand up from a sitting position, move its arms, bow, and speak. Its power and movement came from an electric motor, pulley, cables, and levers hidden in its body, along with a second electric motor hidden in the platform it stood on.

That same year, Japanese writer and biologist Nishimura Makoto introduced the world to his nation's first robot, named Gakutensoku. This stationary robot sat at a desk. Its head was made of rubber, and its eyes, mouth, cheeks, and neck moved, giving it a natural, expressive face. The robot was capable of writing. It moved by means of air pushed through rubber tubes. This put pressure on various parts, causing them to move. Many other humanoid robots were built and introduced to the world in the early 1900s, but like the automatons that came before them, most were for amusement.

First Autonomous Robot

Not everyone developing robots was making machines that looked liked humans. Neurophysiologist William Grey Walter was looking for ways to better understand animal brains. He came up with the idea of building small machines that modeled basic animal behavior. Walter built two robots in 1948 and 1949 named Elmer and Elsie. Their names came from what they were: Electro Mechanical Robots, Light Sensitive. The robots, often referred to as turtles or tortoises, were covered in

Walter's robots were also known as "cybernetic tortoises."

Today's robotic toys feature sensors much more advanced than those used by Walter's turtles.

clear plastic domes while moving around. Like animals, they could explore their environment "actively, persistently, and systematically."[5]

The robots had two sensors connected to two motors. The first sensor was a photocell that detected light; the second communicated when the turtle's shell bumped into something. The sensors allowed the turtles to move autonomously around a room. The photocell was connected to the drive and steering motors. The robots navigated according to the intensity of light they sensed. When the photocell detected light, the robots moved towards it, but if the light was too bright, the robots would turn away from it. If the turtles met an obstacle they could change directions. They were also able to return to a home base where they could recharge their batteries.

The robots of the early 1900s amused audiences who saw them. Some even fulfilled a few practical purposes. However, they represented only a few small steps compared to the giant leaps in robotics technology that would come in the second half of the century.

The Birth of
MODERN ROBOTS

$$\frac{a+b}{a} = \frac{a}{b} = 1.618$$

R obot development gained momentum in the second half of the 1900s. Science-fiction authors and filmmakers still depicted robots far beyond what scientists were capable of building, but a few of their ideas were beginning to become realities. The invention of integrated circuits made it possible to build smaller, cheaper, faster computers. In turn, this development drove the invention of better robots.

Advances in computers had allowed for computer-aided manufacturing. This type of system makes it possible for computers to control the machines in a factory that cut, shape, and assemble products.

In the 1950s, the Massachusetts Institute of Technology's (MIT) Servomechanisms Laboratory developed a project to make computer-aided manufacturing a reality.

Advances in computers and electronics laid the groundwork for the next generation of robots.

THE TURING TEST

Artificial intelligence is a science that focuses on developing thinking machines. Developing intelligent robots has long been a goal of scientists. In 1950, British mathematician Alan Turing developed a test for these future machines that would determine whether their intelligence and behavior were indistinguishable from those of a human being. In the test, a computer and a human are hidden from view and carry out text conversations with the test administrator. If the administrator is unable to tell which is the human and which is the computer, the computer is said to have passed the Turing test. Many smart machines have been developed since Turing's time, including ones that can translate languages and recognize speech and handwriting. By 2014, however, none had passed the Turing test.

The programming language they created was known as automatically programmed tools (APT). APT was used to program milling machine operations. At a demonstration, the machines automatically produced ashtrays for everyone in attendance. The aerospace, automotive, and electronics industries were early adopters of the technology, but it would take several years before computers were reliable and fast enough for the technology to be more widely used.

Intelligent Robots

Artificial intelligence was a term first used by Stanford University researcher John McCarthy in a 1955 conference proposal. He called for a conference to discuss artificial intelligence, focusing on the notion that any feature of intelligence or learning should be able to be broken down in such a way that a computer could accomplish it. Eleven years later, in 1966, the Stanford Research Institute's Artificial Intelligence Center (AIC) was founded.

AIC worked on developing a robot called Shakey, introduced in 1972. Considered to be the first autonomous, intelligent robot, Shakey made its own decisions about

Shakey's development was funded by the US military.

how to respond to simple instructions. It was able to observe its environment, move around obstacles, and perform simple tasks, such as rearranging objects. A 1970 *LIFE* magazine article called Shakey the "first electronic person."[1]

Early Industrial Robots

Although science-fiction stories tend to focus on humanoid robots, it is nonhuman robots that were first developed and used for practical purposes. In 1948, at the Argonne National Laboratory in Chicago, Raymond Goertz developed the "master-slave," a telerobotic arm.[2] A telerobotic device is one that is controlled remotely by a human rather than being capable of completely independent movement. The master-slave's job was to handle radioactive materials while its operator was situated in a safe area.

In 1954, a mostly self-taught inventor named George Devol applied for a patent for a robotic mechanical arm. It could be programmed to perform a series of repetitive tasks, such as picking up something and moving it to another location. Devol called the concept *universal automation*. Sometime later, Devol met engineer Joseph Engelberger at a cocktail party. Devol described his invention to Engelberger, who immediately understood its importance. In 1956, inspired by Devol's invention, Engelberger formed the first robotics company, Unimation Corporation. *Unimation* is a shortened version of *universal automation*.

Around the same time, another company called Planet Corporation had developed a robot called Planobot. Its purpose was to move dangerously hot parts from a die-casting machine to other areas of a manufacturing facility. Only a few were ever built, and due to lack of sales, production was discontinued.

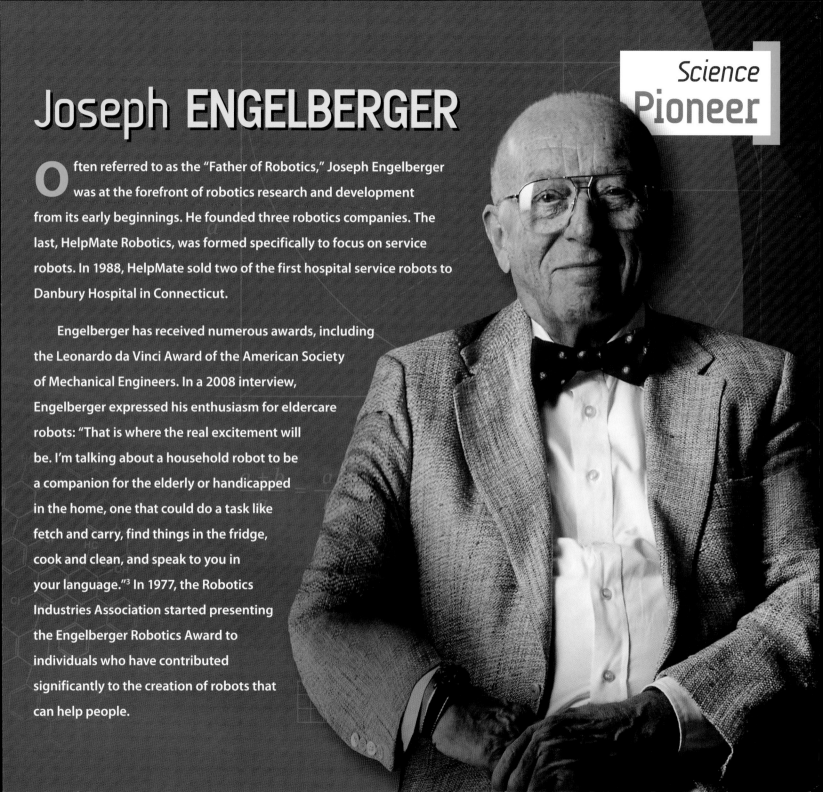

Joseph ENGELBERGER

Often referred to as the "Father of Robotics," Joseph Engelberger was at the forefront of robotics research and development from its early beginnings. He founded three robotics companies. The last, HelpMate Robotics, was formed specifically to focus on service robots. In 1988, HelpMate sold two of the first hospital service robots to Danbury Hospital in Connecticut.

Engelberger has received numerous awards, including the Leonardo da Vinci Award of the American Society of Mechanical Engineers. In a 2008 interview, Engelberger expressed his enthusiasm for eldercare robots: "That is where the real excitement will be. I'm talking about a household robot to be a companion for the elderly or handicapped in the home, one that could do a task like fetch and carry, find things in the fridge, cook and clean, and speak to you in your language."[3] In 1977, the Robotics Industries Association started presenting the Engelberger Robotics Award to individuals who have contributed significantly to the creation of robots that can help people.

A patent was issued to Devol in 1961 for the concept of automated robotic arms. In the same year, a device called the Unimate was installed in a General Motors automobile manufacturing plant in Ewing Township, New Jersey. The Unimate was programmed to move hot metal and perform welding tasks. General Motors did not, however, publicize its new robotic workers. Despite the fact the Unimate was doing highly dangerous work most humans did not want to do, labor unions resisted the introduction of robots because they were concerned human jobs would be lost. By 1966, both Ford and Chrysler had robots in their plants. They welded, spray-painted, and applied adhesives.

In 1968, Unimation licensed its robot technology to Kawasaki Heavy Industries of Japan. US factories were slow to adopt robots, but Japanese manufacturers were quick to seize the advantages robotics presented. Japan was facing a shortage of workers, and it saw robots as a solution to its problem. This marked the beginning of Japan's sizable robot industry.

Carnegie Mellon

The Robotics Institute at Carnegie Mellon University opened its doors in 1979. It was a collaboration of two professors, Raj Reddy and Angel Jordan, and the president of Westinghouse, Thomas J. Murrin. The founders dreamed of ushering in a new age of thinking robots. It was the first robotics department in any US university. The Robotics Institute has seen many achievements since it first formed, and it has been at the forefront of robotics research and development. Its research volume has doubled every seven years since 1979.[4]

Unimate robotic arms were controversial among workers when introduced.

The Integrated Circuit

In 1958, when Texas Instruments employee Jack Kilby invented the integrated circuit, he had no idea what impact it would have on the future of electronics. His idea of putting all the components of an electronic device onto a semiconductor allowed for a huge reduction in the size and power requirements of electronic devices. Semiconductors are materials that work as both conductors and inhibitors of electrons. When Kilby overlaid the metal parts needed to connect many different pieces of circuitry on top of the semiconductor, the integrated circuit was born.

The compact size of the integrated circuits allowed for portability, meaning they could be used in any size device, anywhere. They would also prove relatively inexpensive to make. As Kilby noted many years later, "What we didn't realize then was that the integrated circuit would reduce the cost of electronic functions by a factor of a million to one."[5]

In an interview with the *New York Times*, Intel Corporation cofounder Gordon Moore described the impact of the integrated circuit on electronics by comparing it to the automotive industry: "If the auto industry advanced as rapidly as the semiconductor industry, a Rolls-Royce would get a half a million miles per gallon, and it would be cheaper to throw it away than to park it."[6]

Modern integrated circuits now house millions of microscopically small components on a single fingernail-sized wafer. They can be found everywhere. They are in phones, video game consoles, televisions, and millions of other products and devices. The computer revolution would not have happened and the Internet would not exist if not for the integrated circuit. The integrated circuit paved the way for massive advances in the field of robotics.

Kilby's 1958 prototype of an integrated circuit was crude compared to today's computer chips.

Industrial
ROBOTS

$$\frac{a+b}{a} = \frac{a}{b} = 1,618$$

Industrial robots have come a long way since the Unimate was first used in industrial settings. From automotive assembly and metal fabrication plants to electronics and packaging factories, if there is a dangerous, dirty, heavy, or precise repetitive task to be done, chances are a robot is doing all or part of the job.

An industrial robot is a machine that can be reprogrammed and automatically controlled to perform industrial tasks. A reprogrammable robot is one whose motions or functions can be changed without making physical changes to the robot itself. A multipurpose robot is one that can be adapted for more than one use.

Robots have become integral to the construction of modern cars.

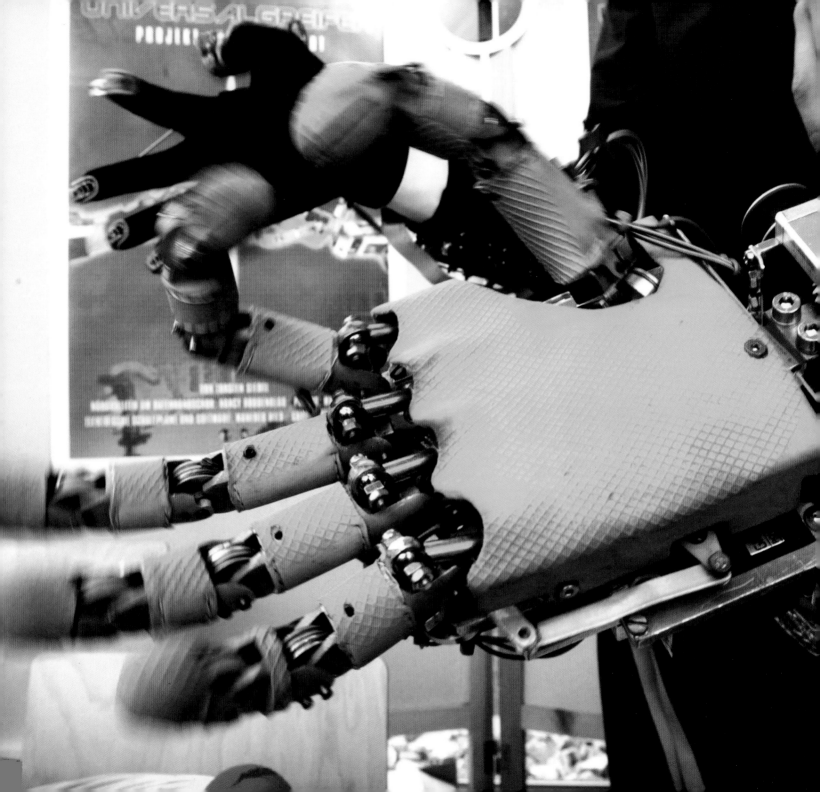

Robot Arms

Robot arms are the most commonly found robots in industrial settings. They can be fitted with different end effectors or specialized "hands" to perform specific jobs. End effectors are also sometimes called accessories, peripherals, or tools. Types of end effectors include grippers, welding guns, vacuum pumps, blowtorches, and drills. They are programmed to carry out a complex series of activities from picking and moving parts to welding, painting, and drilling. This was not always the case, however. It took years of trial and error before robot arms were able to perform consistently, efficiently, and precisely.

One objective of those developing robotic arms was to recreate the movement of a human arm and hand. This was no easy task. The human wrist, for example, has three degrees of freedom. It has the ability to move up and down, side to side, and rotationally. Increasing the degrees of freedom in robotic arms was key to increasing their diversity of use. The late 1960s and 1970s were a time of rapid development for industrial robot arms.

DEGREES OF FREEDOM

Degrees of freedom are used to describe a robot's freedom of motion. The degrees refer to the directions in which the robot can move. A tilting up-and-down motion is called *pitch*, a swiveling side-to-side movement is called *yaw*, and a rotating motion is called *roll*. Robotic arms can also usually translate, or move up and down, left and right, and forward and backward without rotation. Still, these movements are somewhat clumsy compared to human movement, because human hands have 27 degrees of freedom. This allows for an enormous amount of coordination and dexterity, something a robotic manipulator with an end effector cannot match.[1]

Creating robotic hands capable of matching the flexibility of human ones is among the biggest challenges in robotics.

AUTOMATED GUIDED VEHICLE SYSTEM

Another innovative automated device of the 1950s that would foreshadow the future is the automatic guided vehicle (AGV). Developed by the Barrett Electronics Corporation, the AGV is a driverless electric cart used to pull heavy loads in warehouses. The early systems worked much like toy racetracks. A series of wires was laid into the concrete floor of the warehouse. Sensors in the cart looked for and followed the magnetic field created by the wires. This technology was used through the 1970s, until AGVs started using microprocessors that allowed for small, sophisticated computers placed on board to communicate with and manage the system directly.

In 1968, Marvin Minsky of MIT built an octopus-like tentacle arm for the US Office of Naval Research to use in underwater exploration. The arm had 12 joints with a single degree of freedom in each.[2] Victor Scheinman developed the Stanford arm, featuring six degrees of freedom, in 1969. Two years later, Cincinnati-based company Milacron began marketing its computer-controlled industrial robot, The Tomorrow Tool, also known as T3. MIT was up next with its Silver Arm. Developed by David Silver and introduced in 1974, the arm used touch and pressure sensors and a microcomputer to perform precise assembly jobs.

It was also in 1974 that Scheinman formed Vicarm Inc. to manufacture robotic arms. The following year, his Stanford arm succeeded in tests of automotive manufacturing tasks. By 1978, Scheinman had taken his computer control system a step further. Working with Unimation for General Motors, he developed the programmable universal machine for assembly (PUMA). PUMA was able to assemble small car components such as lights and dash panels. All these machines were the ancestors to the nearly 160,000 industrial robots that were sold worldwide in 2012.[3]

Advances in the 1970s made robot arms capable of more precise, delicate tasks than ever before.

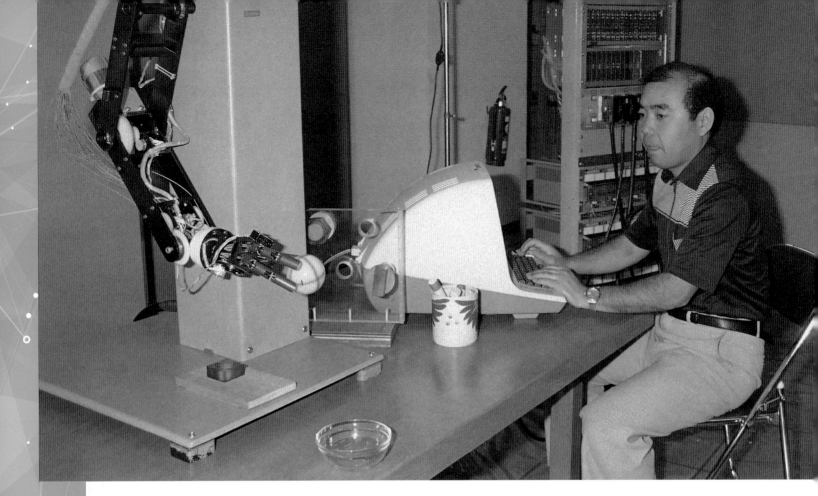

Japan has been a key center of robotics research for more than three decades.

Robotic Workforce

The size of the industrial robotic workforce has vastly increased in the last several decades. The automotive industry, in particular, drove growth in the United States. General Motors installed spot-welding robots in its plants, automating 90 percent of body welding operations and shifting this dangerous job away from human workers.[4] It was not long before Daimler-Benz in Germany installed its own welding line with robots in 1971. The following year, both Fiat in Italy and Nissan in Japan were using robots on spot-welding production lines.

In 1981, Takeo Kanade, a Japanese scientist at the Robotics Institute at Carnegie Mellon University, designed the Direct Drive Robotic Arm. This innovation allowed for smoother, quicker, and more precise movement of robotic arms, opening their use up for more applications. Over the next 30 years, companies started using robots in all kinds of manufacturing plants. In addition to welding in automotive plants, robots can be found in the factories of furniture company Ikea, in foundries handling hot metal castings, and in factories molding plastic packaging. You can find robots painting, picking parts, or assembling small electronic components. By 2013, the top nine robot-using countries had almost 1 million robots in operation. Japan had almost one-third of these, with more than 310,000.[5]

DIRECT DRIVE ROBOTIC ARM

When Kanade designed the Direct Drive Robotic Arm in 1981, it improved the performance of robot arms. Prior to his invention, robotic arms used drive chains to transfer power from the motor to the robot's joints. The bulky chain drives produced uneven movement and were prone to breaking. Direct Drive Robotic Arms have motors built inside each joint, eliminating the need for chains. This allows for robotic arms to move more freely, smoothly, and precisely. Kanade continued to work on his design and soon developed the Direct Drive Arm II. It featured six degrees of freedom, allowing for a wider range of motion and more precise manipulation. The Direct Drive Arm II was donated to the Computer History Museum in California in the late 1980s.

Industrial robots continue to evolve. A number of factors drive their research and development, including energy efficiency, global competitiveness, growing consumer markets, and concerns about worker safety. One area of robotics, in particular, that is expected to grow in manufacturing is human-machine collaboration. Robots in this area are capable of understanding voices, gestures, or graphic instructions. They have components that will allow users to program and integrate the robot to work side by side with human coworkers.

Many modern factories feature cooperation between robots and their human coworkers.

Chapter Six

Research and Service ROBOTS

$$\frac{a+b}{a} = \frac{a}{b} = 1{,}618$$

While robots were being developed to work in factories, scientists were also working on robots to move beyond industry for use in a wide range of fields and applications. From outer space and the deep oceans to hospital rooms and homes, robots started popping up almost everywhere.

Few work environments are more hostile to human beings than the cold vacuum of space. Robots were a logical choice for early space missions, and they continue to be used today. The first robots in space were satellites. Beginning in 1957, the Soviet Union and the United States competed to launch advanced satellites. Since then, a wide variety of robots have been launched to explore our universe.

There are several different types of space robots. They include orbital satellites, landers and rovers, anthrobots, and robonauts. Orbital satellites gather information

Canada's Dextre robot helps maintain and repair the International Space Station.

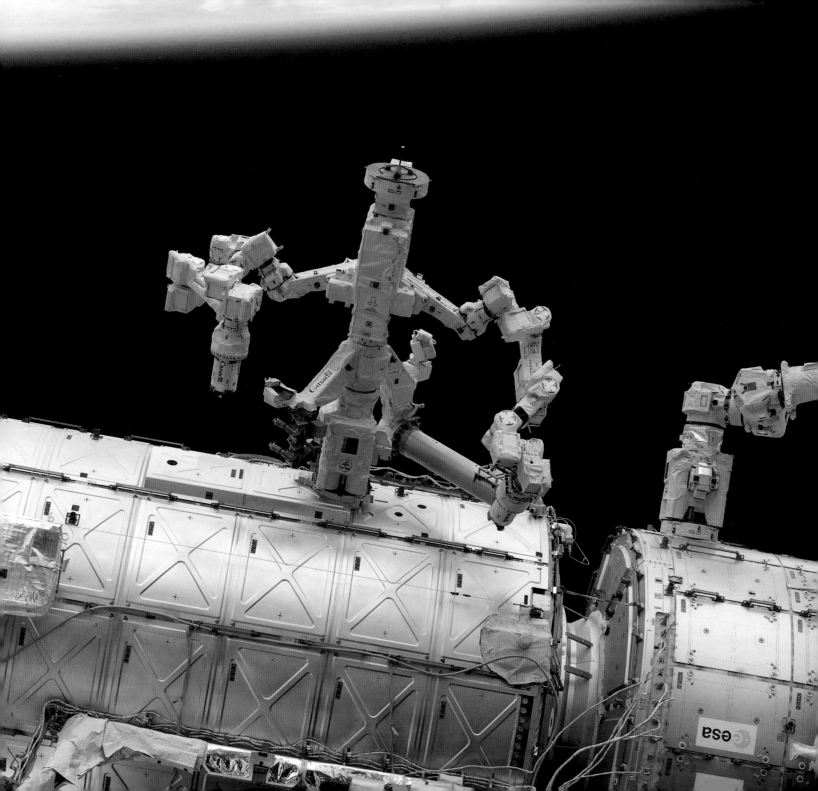

CANADARM

The Canadarm is one of the most successful space robots of all time. It took seven years to develop. The Canadarm has two rotating joints at the shoulder, one at the elbow, and three at the wrist. It is 49 feet (15 m) long. It weighs only 1,058 pounds (480 kg) but is capable of moving more than 70,000 pounds (30,000 kg) using less electricity than a plug-in teakettle.[3] It can be operated by an astronaut or programmed to function automatically. Between its debut on November 13, 1981, and the retirement of the space shuttle program in 2011, the Canadarm was deployed dozens of times. It carried out many diverse tasks, from removing ice on the space shuttle to helping the shuttle dock to a Russian space station. It has captured and repaired satellites, maintained equipment, and moved cargo. The Canadarm was the first of several Canadian space robots. Its successors include the Canadarm2, which is permanently docked at the International Space Station, and Dextre, a robot that helps repair and maintain the station.

from space and then transmit it back to Earth. They serve many purposes, including supporting communication networks, monitoring weather, and tracking changes to Earth's surface. The first US satellite, *Explorer I*, was launched January 31, 1958. Its purpose was to measure radiation levels in Earth's orbit. It sent transmissions back to Earth for 112 days before its battery died.[1] The Hubble Space Telescope is another example of an orbital satellite. Launched in April 1990, this space-based optical telescope has cameras turned away from Earth to observe and photograph the universe. It transmits 120 gigabytes of data every week back to Earth.[2]

Landers and rovers are sent beyond Earth's orbit to land on other planets, such as Mars and Venus. They explore the surfaces of these planets, study their atmospheres, and look for signs of life. One US rover, *Opportunity*, was launched on June 10, 2003, and landed on Mars on January 3, 2004. The robotic rover is equipped with a panoramic camera, microscopic imager, navigation camera, and hazard avoidance cameras, among other tools and sensors. Its mission was only supposed to last three months. In the summer of 2014, more than ten years later, it was still going

The *Curiosity* rover is capable of autonomously navigating around obstacles on the Martian surface.

DA VINCI'S SPACE ROBOT

Leonardo da Vinci's drawings of the human body are still considered amazingly precise for their time. More than 500 years after he put them to paper, NASA used the drawings to help design their first humanoid robot. American robotics expert Mark Rosheim studied and applied the information in da Vinci's drawings to design and produce a model anthrobot for NASA. Rosheim said, "His anatomical drawings are unique and they gave me the information I needed to emulate the complex joints and muscles of the human body."[4] Anthrobot is a term first used by Rosheim in a paper he presented to a robotics conference in 1990. The word anthrobotics comes from anthropomorphic, meaning having human characteristics, combined with robotic. The term anthrobot is used to distinguish the new generation of dexterous robots from their simpler ancestors.

strong and sending information back to the US National Aeronautics and Space Administration (NASA).

The rover *Spirit* landed on the opposite side of Mars from *Opportunity* on January 4, 2004. It is equipped with special tools to study the rocks and soils on Mars, including instruments for analyzing composition and mineral content. NASA landed a new Mars rover named *Curiosity* on August 5, 2012. This car-sized, six-wheeled rover is on a mission to find out if Mars is habitable.

The United States is not alone in sending robots to space. In December 2013, the China National Space Administration achieved the first landing on the moon in 37 years. The Chang'e-3 lander and the Yutu rover it deployed were used to study the geography of their landing spot.

Anthrobots are robots whose dexterity and flexibility resembles that of a human, although the robot itself may not look human. The arms and hands of anthrobots have multiple degrees of freedom, enabling them to perform tasks as well as an astronaut dressed in a space suit.

Robonauts, on the other hand, are built to look like humans. NASA has developed and continues to improve on these dexterous, humanoid robots. Their humanoid shape is necessary because existing spacecraft are designed to be serviced by human astronauts. The robonauts will be able to fit into the same spaces, perform the same maneuvers, and use the same tools as astronauts, while at the same time putting the human crew at a much lower risk.

Ocean Explorers

The deep ocean is just as hazardous to people as outer space. Among the earliest human-occupied vehicles to go for a deep dive was the *Alvin* in 1964. The vessel was equipped with robotic arms the human operators onboard could manipulate to pick up things from the ocean floor. However, diving so deep with humans aboard is always risky. Explorers developed remotely operated vehicles (ROVs) to carry out deep, long-duration trips. These robots are attached to a ship. Inside the ship, a scientist operates the robot by remote control.

The development of autonomous underwater vehicles (AUVs) began in the 1960s. Unlike ROVs, these vessels are not tethered to ships. They travel out on their own to gather data, then transmit the information back to the scientists. In 2009, an AUV named *Nereus* dove 6.8 miles (11 km) to reach the deepest part of Earth's oceans, the Mariana Trench.[5] Robots have made it possible to reach the farthest depths of

US Navy AUVs often have sleek shapes, allowing them to move efficiently through water.

the ocean and the outermost reaches of our solar system without subjecting human explorers to risk.

Medical Robots

Advances in industrial and space robots paved the way for one of the newest and most promising fields of robotics: medical robots. Robots are now being used for a number of rehabilitation, therapy, and surgery applications, as well as other specialized medical needs.

In 1985, the first robotic surgery took place when Yik San Kwoh, director of research in the radiology department at the Long Beach Memorial Medical Center in California, used a computerized robotic arm to assist with brain surgery. The device held and directed a surgical drill and biopsy needle, while the doctors applied pressure on the instruments to penetrate the skull and brain. At the time, Kwoh said that the PUMA 560 robotic arm's extreme accuracy "eliminated the need for general anesthesia, reduced trauma to the brain, and allowed patients to go home the day after brain surgery instead of a week or more later."[6] Laparoscopic surgery was also being developed at this time. Laparoscopic surgery is minimally invasive surgery that involves the surgeon inserting an instrument called a trocar into small incisions in the patient. Specialized instruments and a miniature camera are passed through the trocars. The camera transmits images from the patient's abdomen to high-resolution video monitors in the operating room. This allows the surgeon to perform the same operations as before but with much smaller incisions. The first laparoscopic surgery to remove a gallbladder was performed by French surgeon Dr. Philippe Mouret in 1987.

In 1992, International Business Machines developed a prototype robot to assist with orthopaedic surgery. Its robot, named ROBODOC, was used during hip replacement operations to mill out a hole in the femur. And in 1998, Dr. David Gow developed the first bionic arm, called the Edinburgh Modular Arm System.

EKSO

One of the most exciting developments in medical robotics is the exoskeleton, a wearable bionic suit. Several companies are working on different types of exoskeletons, but Ekso Bionics was the first to debut its suit to the public in 2010. The suit gives any individual with lower limb mobility impairment the ability to stand and walk. For the first time ever, people with spinal cord injuries, poststroke paralysis, or immobility due to traumatic brain injury are able to walk. The Ekso is a gait-training tool meant to be used under the supervision of a physical therapist. The suit is strapped on over the user's clothing and walking is achieved by the user shifting his or her weight. The weight shift activates sensors in the device, which then initiates steps. The legs of the Ekso are driven by battery-powered motors. Since its debut, the Ekso has taken more than 1 million steps.[7]

One of the early rehabilitation robots, its purpose was to help individuals with severe disabilities live more independently. Rehabilitation robotics focuses on robots that can help people recover from severe injuries or provide assistance to those who have special needs. There are now a number of different kinds of rehabilitation robots. Assistive robots allow people with disabilities to live more independently. They assist with simple tasks such as eating, drinking, and opening doors. Smart wheelchairs and walkers feature intelligent navigation systems to help those with lower limb and visual impairments. Robotic prostheses now replace lost limbs, and robotic orthotics support injured or weak limbs, giving mobility back to those who have lost it.

It was telepresence technology, however, that brought about some of the most amazing medical robots. Several organizations, including the Stanford Research Institute, the US Department of Defense, and NASA, were all researching ways to develop telepresence technology that would allow surgeons to perform operations from a distance. Their goal was to mount a robotic arm on armored vehicles to provide immediate surgical care to wounded soldiers on

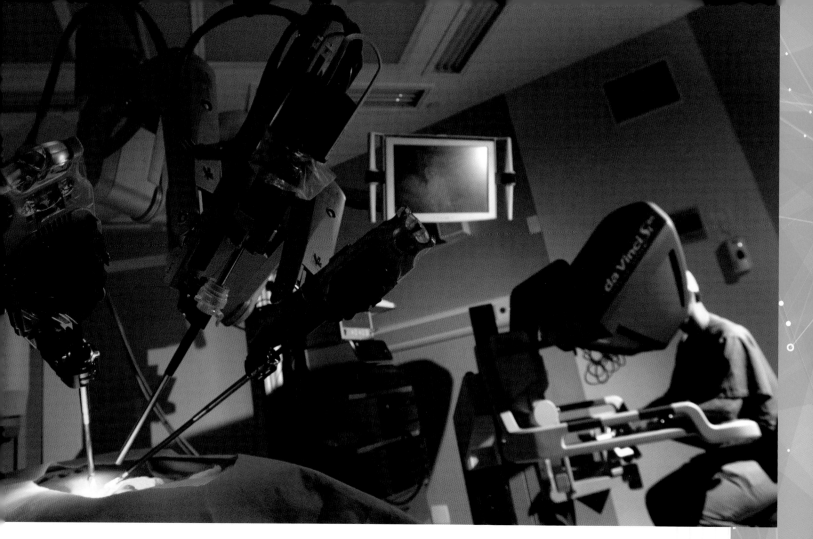

The da Vinci Surgical System is controlled by a surgeon sitting at a control console.

the battlefield. This research led to Intuitive Surgical's development of the da Vinci Surgical System. The da Vinci Surgical System robot is among the most popular surgical robots in use. With this robot assistant, surgeons only need to make a few small cuts to allow for the insertion of a tiny camera and miniature tools. Then, the surgeon takes the controls and looks at a monitor showing live video of the inside of the patient. The latest version of the system takes three-dimensional, high-definition video to give surgeons a clear view of the surgery site.

Many surgical robot assistants have been developed since the da Vinci. They now help with brain, heart, and kidney surgeries. The neuroArm, for example, assists doctors with very delicate brain surgery. Patients remain in a magnetic resonance imaging (MRI) machine during the operation. The MRI provides a three-dimensional image of the brain. Doctors control the robot arm from another room while watching what they are doing on a screen. This machine is an example of how telepresence technology has allowed surgeons to perform surgery from a distant location. They can be across the room or even across the country.

Domestic Robots

Domestic robots have much less dramatic jobs than those that explore space, dive into the ocean, or assist with life-saving surgeries. However, these robots are the most common in everyday life. They make mundane daily tasks easier, freeing their owners from chores and allowing them to spend more time on more interesting activities. The first domestic robots were simple robotic vacuums, such as iRobot's Roomba, which was launched in 2002. The company, founded by Rodney Brooks, has been a pioneer in the field of domestic robots. Its Roombas had a striking resemblance to

Rodney BROOKS

R odney Brooks's name is tied to some of the most well known robots of modern times. In 1990, along with two other MIT roboticists, Brooks formed the company iRobot. The company's best known robot is the Roomba, but iRobot has been developing all kinds of robots since its inception. In 1998, it was awarded a contract by DARPA to build a tactical mobile robot; this led to the development of the PackBot. The company has introduced a new robot almost every year since. By 2013, iRobot had sold more than 5,000 defense and security robots and more than 10 million home robots.[8] Since 1993, Brooks has also been the director of the MIT Computer Science and Artificial Intelligence Laboratory. He was the founder of the Cog Project, whose aim is to construct a humanoid robot that is capable of fine, precise movements and can be used for many tasks. By 2014, iRobot was a household name, and the Cog Project was still going strong.

the automated light-sensitive robots Elmer and Elsie built by Walter in the late 1940s.

Like Walter's turtles, robot vacuums can move autonomously around a room and return to their base stations to recharge their batteries. The robots automatically adapt to different floor surfaces, and they have sensors that prevent them from running into walls or tumbling down staircases. Variants of the Roomba have been developed by iRobot to serve as lawn mowers and pool cleaners. Unlike industrial robots, which can be reprogrammed or reconfigured to perform multiple tasks, these domestic robots are typically designed to perform only a single task. Still, amateur robot enthusiasts frequently take apart domestic robots and reprogram them for new uses.

Security robots are also being used in more places. They come in a variety of shapes and sizes. Security robots have wide-angle cameras with night vision. Their camera heads are attached to wheeled bases. These robots have the ability to navigate around homes and property, detect intruders, record video, and communicate this information to their owners via text message or e-mail.

FURBY

Around the same time robotic vacuum cleaners were being introduced to households, robotic interactive toys were being introduced to children. In 1998, Tiger Electronics debuted its artificial pet, Furby. Furby was an odd-looking creature that stood approximately eight inches (20 cm) tall and had synthetic fur.[9] It had a beak and oversized eyes and ears, all of which had the ability to move when it spoke or in response to its owner's voice. Furby could express its feelings, give kisses, sing, and dance. It even spoke its own language. When it came into contact with another Furby, the two could communicate with each other. Although very simple compared to later robots, Furby was a huge hit with kids and adults alike. Approximately 40 million of the toys were sold.[10]

Security robots are capable of patrolling areas and alerting authorities in case of theft, fire, or other emergencies.

The Double telepresence robot balances on two wheels as it moves around.

In 2006, Chinese robotics experts introduced a robot security guard. Jointly developed by the Civil Aviation University of China and Tianjin Ya'an Technology Electronics, the robot looks like a small car. It uses cameras and ultrasonic sensors to send information back to a central control station. The GrounBot by Rotundus of Belgium, the SECOM Robot X out of Japan, and the Avatar III from Robotex are just a few of the other models of security robots now available on the market.

Home telepresence robots are basically computer monitors with video cameras, microphones, and speakers, all attached to a stand on wheels. They are relatively new, and a number of companies are rushing to get them to corporate and consumer markets. A telepresence robot allows a person to virtually be in two places at once. Double Robotics' telepresence robot, called Double, is essentially a mount on wheels that with an iPad attached can be navigated around an office or home. For example, a mother can connect to her Double robot at home to check on her kids while she is at work. Her children would see her face on the iPad screen and hear her voice through the speakers. The mother can move the robot around her home remotely. She can see her home and children through the video camera, and her children can talk to her directly through the microphone. She can be present even when she is not at home.

The Beam+ developed by Suitable Technologies is similar, except it has three wheels and its own screen. The company has also priced the robot to be affordable for the average consumer. Another robot, Ava, developed by iRobot in partnership with Cisco Systems, is the first self-driving telepresence robot. Ava debuted in

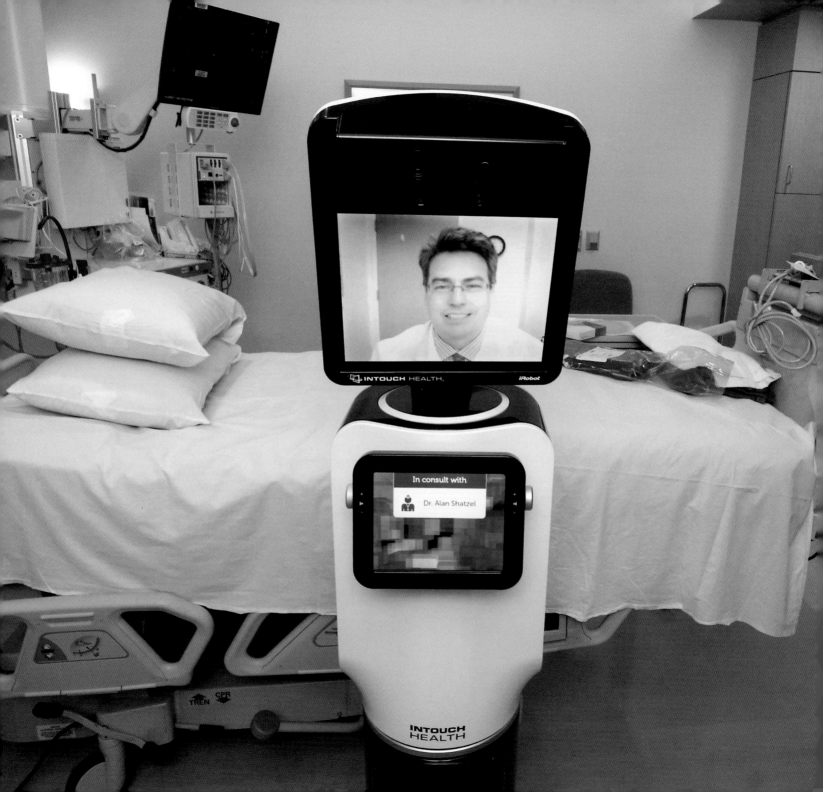

In consult with

Dr. Alan Shatzel

June 2013. It has the ability to avoid obstacles, including people, while driving autonomously to a destination. It is being marketed to large businesses to use for facility tours and inspections, remote training and presentations, and employee collaboration. The interest in these kinds of robots continues growing. At the same time, many developers are trying to bring the price of the units down. These two factors combined make it likely telepresence robots will become part of everyday life in the coming years, whether at home, work, or school.

Telepresence robots are now finding use in the medical field.

Rescue and War
ROBOTS

$$\frac{a+b}{a} = \frac{a}{b} = 1,618$$

Military and rescue robots can be classified in three categories: unmanned marine vehicles (UMVs); unmanned ground vehicles (UGVs); and unmanned aerial vehicles (UAVs), also called drones. They come in a wide range of shapes and sizes and are capable of performing a vast number of tasks, from reconnaissance to rescue to actual combat.

Radio- and remote-controlled vehicles were used by various military forces in both World War I (1914–1918) and World War II (1939–1945) and again by the United States in the Vietnam War (1955–1973). It was not until the late 1970s, however, that the US military began investing heavily in robotics research and development.

In 1979, the US Army committed $560 million to developing and building 780 Lockheed Aquilas.[1] The Aquila was a small, propeller-powered, remotely piloted UAV.

Militaries use a wide variety of rugged robots.

Its purpose was to fly over enemy front lines and send back information to troops on the ground. The army soon envisioned other purposes for the Aquila, and it started asking for new features, including night vision. Each new feature increased the budget, and eventually the program was scrapped with only a few prototypes ever built. It was a glimpse, however, of what the future would hold.

The 1990s brought two advances that helped increase the acceptance of military robot technology. First, computers became faster and smaller, making it possible to build lightweight unmanned vehicles that still possessed the large amount of processing power needed to handle inputs from many sensors. The second advance was the Global Positioning System (GPS), which the government began building in the 1970s but did not finish until the mid-1990s. GPS is a navigation system composed of dozens of orbiting satellites. Handheld GPS receivers on the ground receive signals from multiple satellites at once. By comparing the time it takes for signals from different satellites to reach the receiver, the receiver's location can be calculated. The military realized it could place GPS receivers inside unmanned vehicles, making it possible to accurately track their location and control them remotely from thousands of miles away. The US military committed itself to investing in new robotic technologies.

Predator UAVs contain sophisticated sensors and communications equipment.

Unmanned Aerial Vehicles

UAVs have advanced a great deal since the Aquila project was scrapped. They come in a variety of sizes ranging from large blimps to micro-helicopters. The most common use for UAVs is reconnaissance. For example, a spy balloon called an aerostat was used in Afghanistan to survey outposts and send back live video to forces on the ground from as far away as 20 miles (32 km).[2]

The Predator is among the most recognizable drones. If a photograph of a UAV is used in the media, it is usually a picture of the Predator. The Predator's cameras and sensors are linked to global communications systems. This allows a pilot to remotely fly it from any location in the world, using a joystick and computer screen. The drones can be armed with missiles, though they cannot fire them without input from the pilot. The use of Predators and other UAVs has grown substantially. In 2001, the US military had fewer than 50 UAVs. By 2011, it had more than 7,000. The US Air Force now trains more UAV pilots than fighter and bomber pilots combined.[3]

Several other countries develop UAVs as well. The tiny Penguin B developed by Latvian company UAV Factory set a 54.5-hour world endurance record for its size class.[4] Israeli company Elbit Systems also develops a number of UAVs. Their Hermes 450 UAVs have more than 300,000 operational flight hours.[5] Their next-generation Hermes 900 can also assist with ground support and participate in patrol missions over water.

Unmanned Ground Vehicles

One of the most widely used types of military robots is the UGV. They come in all shapes and sizes; their versatility makes them well-suited for military purposes. A basic model includes audio-video recording devices and a mechanical arm. They can be adapted with a number of features, including chemical, gas, radiation, and temperature sensors. They are built to be tough and meant to go almost anywhere.

The US military's Ripsaw UGV can lay mines and tow disabled vehicles.

They can climb stairs, navigate rubble, and manage deep snow. Not all UGVs are small. Large military UGVs resemble trucks or tanks. They are equipped with onboard computers, so they can be operated remotely. They can do everything from sweeping for land mines and cutting down obstacles to towing disabled vehicles and hauling cargo.

The earliest use of UGVs in a war zone was in 2000, following the Bosnian War (1992–1995). A robot was used to move and dispose of live grenades left over from the conflict. Two years later, robots went where no US soldier would want to go: into the network of caves in Afghanistan thought to be hiding enemy personnel and weapons. Remotely operated, the robots were sent into the caves in front of soldiers to assess the area for safety. The four robots were small but tough. They were designed to meet certain criteria. They had to be heavy enough to trigger a land mine, tall enough to trip a booby-trap line, and long enough to carry cameras and a 12-gauge shotgun.

Considering the previous battlefield success of UGVs, US forces were somewhat slow to use them when they invaded Iraq in 2003. It did not take long for things to change, though. Within a year, the forces had implemented approximately 150 robots. By the end of 2005, there were 2,400 robots on the ground in Iraq.[6] Three years later, there were approximately 12,000 UGVs of various shapes, sizes, and purposes helping soldiers in a number of ways.[7] If a person was injured or killed by a bomb, it was a tragedy. But if a robot got blown up, it was a good thing. In 2004, after a PackBot was blown up in Iraq, iRobot executive Colin Angle cheered publicly: "It was

In addition to its UMVs, the US Navy has the capability to launch UAVs from its ships.

a special moment, a robot got blown up instead of a person."[8] There are now dozens of countries around the globe that develop UGVs, including Novatiq in Switzerland, Clearpath Robotics in Canada, and DOK-ING in Croatia.

Unmanned Marine Vehicles

Military forces are also using UMVs more widely than in previous years. Some are fully autonomous, while others are remotely controlled by radio, satellite, or cable communication. The US military identifies four size classifications, ranging from small vehicles that weigh as little as 25 pounds (11 kg) and can be easily carried to large vehicles weighing up to 20,000 pounds (9,000 kg).[9] The US Navy uses these vehicles for many purposes, including surveillance, antisubmarine warfare, scientific missions, and delivering cargo. By 2012, the US military had 450 UMVs in its inventory.[10]

Other nations also see important uses for UMVs. The Republic of Singapore Navy (RSN) believes UMVs will make their navy more effective and efficient. In 2005, the RSN deployed Protector UMVs for maritime security. Equipped with remote-control machine guns and loudspeakers, the vehicles patrolled the waters around an oil terminal to protect it from terrorist attacks. Canada, with the world's longest coastline but a relatively small population and navy, also sees an important role for UMVs. The vehicles can enhance the reach of small navies at a much lower cost than fielding full-size ships filled with trained sailors.

Rescue Robots

Many of the robots designed for military applications have also been used for civilian emergency and rescue purposes. Since September 11, 2001, finding robots at disaster sites or high-risk emergency situations has become increasingly common. Between 2001 and 2012, unmanned robots were used dozens of times at disaster sites to help emergency responders. They have been deployed in nine different countries, including the United States, after natural disasters such as hurricanes, floods, and earthquakes. They have also played a part in rescue efforts following massive explosions and mine collapses. In addition to video cameras, many of these robots are equipped with thermal cameras that can detect the heat of human bodies, smoldering fires, and live electrical outlets. In 2013, there were 300 emergency response teams in the US using robots.[11]

Civilian police forces also use robots. They use UAVs for surveillance and UGVs on bomb-detecting squads. Not only can the robots be adapted to detect explosives, but they are also fitted with tools to disarm them. They can cut wires, lift and grip explosives, and use onboard firearms to detonate bombs. Many US police forces now have bomb-detecting robots. They can be found in airports and at border crossings as well.

Police forces are also using Throwbots. Developed by ReconRobotics, these handy little machines weigh only 1.2 pounds (0.5 kg) and can be thrown up to 120 feet (36 m).[12] Consisting of small boxes with voice and video recorders mounted between two large wheels, these robots can be remotely operated. Users toss a Throwbot over walls and

CHERNOBYL ROBOT FAILURE

On April 26, 1986, one of the reactors at the Chernobyl Nuclear Power Plant in the Soviet Union experienced a catastrophic meltdown. In the aftermath, the Soviet Union was faced with a disaster site that was emitting deadly radiation. More than 100 short tons (90 metric tons) of radioactive debris needed to be cleared from the roof of the reactor.[13] A human worker could spend a maximum of two minutes on the roof before receiving a lethal dose of radiation. The government attempted to use robots to do the work. An open-air museum near the disaster site has some of these robots on display. Most look like bulldozers, cranes, tanks, or a combination of the three. They were sent onto the rooftops to clear debris, but none were able to withstand the radiation. Ultimately the Soviets turned back to people to do the work.

CRASAR

Headed by Dr. Robin Murphy, the Center for Robot-Assisted Search and Rescue (CRASAR) is a research center at Texas A&M University. It operates as both a crisis response and research organization. Its objective is to keep track of all robotics research and development taking place so when a disaster occurs CRASAR has the ability to deploy a team of robots to the site.

Its team deployed robots on-site the day after the September 11, 2001, attacks in New York City and remained there for three weeks. They have deployed robots at dozens of emergencies since then. Their mission is to help existing rescue organizations by providing robot-assisted search and rescue teams. At the same time, they support further research and development of robots that can conduct search and rescue tasks.

around corners to see and hear what is there before they venture forward.

Robots that can traverse virtually any terrain are also being developed. Robotics company Boston Dynamics set out on a mission to build robots that can move over uneven ground and adapt to terrain in the way living creatures do. They made major strides toward this goal with BigDog. Resembling a four-legged giant spider, BigDog can walk, run at four miles per hour (6 kmh), climb 35-degree slopes, and carry loads of up to 340 pounds (154 kg).[14] It can move through rubble, mud, snow, and water without problems.

The BigDog robots are designed to carry supplies alongside soldiers traveling on foot.

Chapter
Eight

The Future of
ROBOTICS

I n the last 50 years, robotics has shifted from trying to catch up with science fiction to outpacing it in many ways. Scientists are working on everything from full-size intelligent humanoid robots to ant-size microbots that can work together to build complex electronics. Advances in robotics are likely to redefine peoples' daily lives.

Medical Service Robots

One of the areas of robotics expected to grow substantially is medical service robots. According to the Population Reference Bureau, the global population of people age 65 and over will reach 1.5 billion by 2050. This will make up 16 percent of the world's population, compared to just 5 percent in 1950.[1] Caring for this aging population is a concern for many governments, and robots may offer one solution to the shortage of eldercare providers.

The HRP-4C robot, designed and built in Japan, has a realistic head and can walk with a natural motion.

$$\frac{a+b}{a} = \frac{a}{b} = 1.618$$

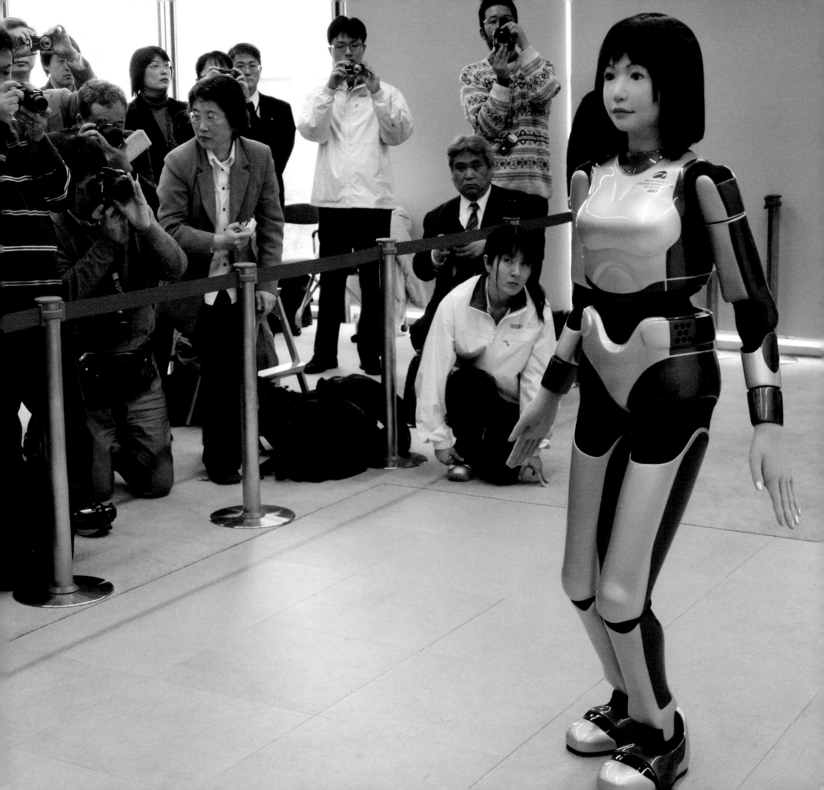

In summer 2011, after an earthquake and tsunami devastated Japan, a social robot called Paro was used to comfort victims. The robot is shaped like a baby seal and was developed by Takanori Shibata at Japan's National Institute of Advanced Industrial Science and Technology in 2003. It is commonly used in nursing homes. Its body is covered in sensors, and it responds to petting by squealing. Studies have shown it can lower stress levels in both users and caregivers.

In spring 2014, a European Union–funded project installed its GiraffPlus robot in the homes of six seniors. The robots are meant to help elderly people who want to continue living alone. Both the seniors and their homes were wired with pressure sensors to track the seniors' mobility. The information collected is fed back to the GiraffPlus, which stores the data. The robot has the ability to do things like monitor blood pressure, check blood-sugar levels, and remind patients to take medications. The GiraffPlus can also operate as a telepresence robot. Family members or health-care workers can call the robot, direct it around the house, and check in on the senior.

Researchers across the globe are experimenting with all kinds of assistive robots. They are working on 24-finger robots that can wash hair and porter robots that can fetch medication and meals. Researchers are also looking at therapy robots that can recommend healthy foods and activities to their users. Robots that can administer speech and object-recognition therapy to patients after strokes are another potential

The Paro robot has been in use
since 2003.

application. These robots are meant to complement human contact rather than replace it entirely.

New Robot Jobs

Researchers are also looking at ways robots can help in the classroom. Robots can take on the role of peer, tutor, or tool. They are most commonly used in language, science, and technology education. Studies have demonstrated students showed more interest and performed better on language tests when learning was done with a robot tutor as opposed to using books or recorded audio of lectures.

A company called Play-i is producing educational robots that teach computer programming concepts and languages through interaction and play. In modern times, learning how to program computers is a valuable skill. Robotics itself would not exist without skilled programmers. Learning to write programming code, however, can be challenging. These new toy robots are engaging kids in a whole new way. They may be training the next generation of robot scientists.

Some of the most promising robots are also among the tiniest. SRI International has built and is testing an army of

ROBOTS FOR AUTISM THERAPY

Autism is a condition characterized by having difficulty communicating and interacting socially. A 2013 study looked at whether robots could assist in therapy sessions. For some children, it may be easier to interact with a simple robot than a human therapist with complex, changing facial expressions. University of Notre Dame psychologist Joshua Diehl noted the robot therapist seemed to improve social skills. Encouraged by these first results, Diehl and his team hope to further develop the robot therapist.

microbots. These antlike robots are steered magnetically. They are capable of moving around obstacles and carrying small items. They can work with metal, glass, wood, and electronic components. They are fast and can climb walls. When combined, they are capable of building structures and objects. Microbots can be reprogrammed to do new tasks, and they are inexpensive. For this reason, it is believed microbots could be an efficient way to build complex devices without having to invest in large-scale production facilities.

Robots have become a standard part of security procedures in many places. UAVs were used at the 2014 Winter Olympic Games in Sochi, Russia, to monitor the events from above. PackBots were used at both the 2014 Winter Olympics and the 2014 FIFA World Cup in Brazil as bomb detectors. This kind of robot security is expected to become popular because robots have the ability to check out potentially dangerous situations without putting humans in danger. Robot security guards are also likely coming soon. Using robots to patrol office towers, parking garages, and shopping malls to assist human workers will

ROBOT STRAWBERRY PICKER

In Japan, strawberries are big business. They are available all year long, but picking them is not easy work. According to Japan's National Agriculture and Food Research Organization, strawberries require 70 times the work of rice farming and twice that of tomatoes and cucumbers. With this in mind, the organization helped develop a robot that could pick strawberries. The robot moves along rails between rows of strawberries grown in raised greenhouse planters. Using three cameras, the robot is able to evaluate the ripeness and color of the strawberry and determine if it is ready for picking. The robot then picks the strawberry and drops it in a basket. It is able to pick one piece of fruit every eight seconds.[2]

be more common. As home security robots become more affordable, they may become mainstream.

Robots by Google

A big influence in the future of robotics is likely to be Google, a company best known for its Internet search engine. In late 2013, Google bought eight companies that develop a broad range of devices related to robot technology.[3] From companies that make robotic arms and manipulators to those that develop electric actuators and industrial sorting robots, Google has purchased the companies it needs to develop all kinds of robots.

Among the companies Google purchased was Boston Dynamics. In addition to BigDog, Boston Dynamics also developed Atlas, a humanoid robot that can negotiate rough outdoor terrain. It can walk on two legs and lift and carry objects. It is coordinated enough to climb on its hands and feet and maneuver its way through crowded spaces. It can handle tools like a human. Its head contains sensors, stereo cameras, and a laser range-finder. Before being acquired by Google, Boston Dynamics had done much of its robotics work for the US military. However, Google has said it will not take military funding for robot development; instead, the company wants to focus on developing commercial products.

Google's driverless cars are gradually becoming legal to use in several US states.

Driverless Cars and Delivery Drones

Robotics will also affect the way we move both people and things. In one of its earliest robotics projects, Google began developing a driverless car in 2009.

The company equipped cars with computers and sensors. Google had to test the new technology secretly at first, because driverless vehicles were neither explicitly allowed nor explicitly banned on US roads. The cars drove thousands of accident-free miles on busy US roads before Google revealed the technology to the world in 2010. Google then overcame a major obstacle when Nevada, California, and Florida passed legislation allowing driverless vehicles on roads. By 2014, approval for driverless cars was also being considered in Hawaii, New Jersey, Oklahoma, and the District of Columbia.

Online shopping giant Amazon.com is another Internet company looking to use robots. Amazon.com CEO Jeff Bezos revealed in December 2013 the company was developing and testing airborne robotic vehicles for delivering small packages directly from Amazon.com warehouses to customers' doors. However, Federal Aviation Administration regulations prohibited the use of such drones for commercial purposes. Until the laws change, delivery UAVs will be banned from the skies.

Robot Fun

Many robot developers simply want to focus on the fun applications of robots. In June 2014, Japanese Internet company SoftBank, along with the French company Aldebaran Robotics and the Taiwanese company Foxconn, unveiled the social robot Pepper. Pepper is the world's first personal robot with the ability to read people's emotions. "We want to have a robot that will maximize people's joy and minimize

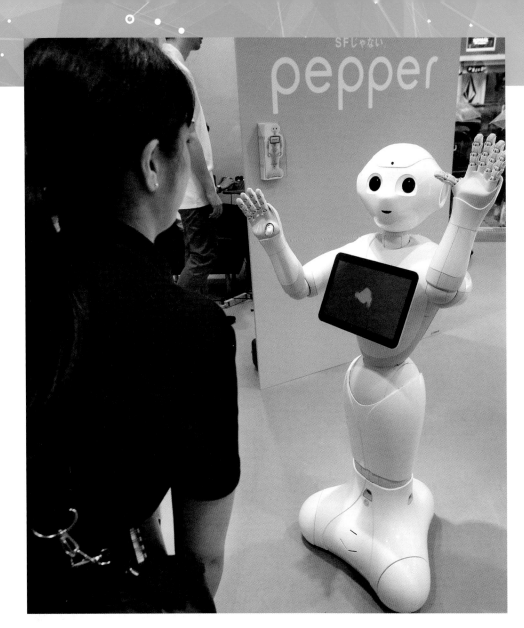

Softbank planned to place Pepper robots in its stores to interact with customers.

their sadness," said SoftBank CEO Masayoshi Son.[4] The company planned to sell it for less than $2,000.[5]

Vendors at the 2014 Toy Fair showcased a wide range of robot toys capable of singing, dancing, shooting, rolling, and more. One six-legged spiderlike robot shoots foam darts. Another robot, called Ozbot, is shaped like a dome and can follow hand-drawn lines on a tablet screen or piece of paper. Differently colored lines correspond to different commands, making it slow down, speed up, or spin. A robot called Romo is making telepresence robots available to the masses. It is a smartphone dock on tank treads. When a person plugs in a smartphone, Romo becomes a smart robot with a customizable personality that is capable of navigating around a home. The Mindstorms robot kits from LEGO allow users to build and program their own robots, then control them using smartphone apps. Toy robots of all kinds are helping train the next generation of robot scientists.

Controversy

With each new development, however, comes potential controversy. The idea that the government might use UAVs to monitor the public raises privacy concerns. Private companies' use of security robots to roam public places and record video also concerns people. Additionally, there are legal and moral controversies surrounding the use of unmanned weapons to strike enemy forces.

In a 2013 report, referring to robots with the ability to kill human beings, United Nations Secretary-General Ban Ki-moon noted that these systems should be designed to work in accordance with human rights laws. In spring 2014, the United Nations held its first-ever convention on these issues. Its stated purpose was to "ban or restrict the use of specific types of weapons that are considered to cause unnecessary or unjustifiable suffering to combatants or to affect civilians indiscriminately."[6]

Ever since their earliest appearances in science fiction, robots have been seen as potentially either dangerous or helpful to society. Today's controversies over robotic drones echo the books and movies that depict robots going haywire and taking over the planet. Yet most uses of robots over the past several decades have been beneficial to society. Robots assemble our cars, explore deep space and the sea, and even provide companionship and assistance in our homes. In the coming years they may be able to carry out autonomous surgery and drive us to work. Robots have become one of the most transformative technologies in our modern society.

ROBOTS CREATE JOBS

In November 2011, marketing firm Metra Martech released a report entitled "Positive Impact of Industrial Robots on Employment." In the report, it predicted that robotics will be a major driver of global job creation through 2020. The data the firm analyzed estimated between 8 and 10 million jobs were created due to robotics through 2008.[7] The report noted that between 2000 and 2008, employment increased in manufacturing in nearly every industrialized country, even while use of robots also increased. The report's author predicts three areas in particular will drive robotics development: robots doing work that is unsafe for humans, robots carrying out tasks more affordably than paying a human worker, and robots doing work that is impossible for humans to do.

Timeline

380 BCE Archytas of Tarentum builds the first-known automaton, a pigeon attached to a bar on a pivot.

150 BCE A Greek ship carrying the Antikythera mechanism sinks.

1490s CE Leonardo da Vinci draws a sketch for a robot knight.

1730s Jacques de Vaucanson builds his complicated mechanical duck, which simulates the process of digestion.

1770 Wolfgang von Kempelen builds the Turk, an apparently automated chess player that turned out to be a hoax.

1801 Joseph Marie Jacquard introduces his new weaving loom, which users could program with punch cards.

1921 Karel Čapek coins the term *robot* in his play *R.U.R.*

1927 Westinghouse introduces the Televox to the world.

1939 Westinghouse introduces Elektro the Moto-Man at the World's Fair in New York City.

1941 In his short story "Liar," science-fiction writer Isaac Asimov coins the term *robotics*.

1948–1949 William Walter Grey builds two robots named Elsie and Elmer.

1961 The first Unimate robot is installed in a General Motors plant in New Jersey.

1966 The Stanford Research Institute's Artificial Intelligence Center (AIC) is founded.

1968 The Unimation Corporation licenses its robot technology to Kawasaki Heavy Industries of Japan.

1972 The AIC builds Shakey the robot.

1981 The Canadian Space Agency debuts the Canadarm.

2001 PackBots and other robots assist rescuers after the September 11 terrorist attacks in New York City.

2002 Robotics company iRobot launches the Roomba vacuum cleaner.

2010 The Ekso, a wearable bionic suit, makes its debut.

2011 Unmanned vehicles are sent to Fukushima Daiichi Nuclear Power Plant in Japan to assess damage following a tsunami.

Essential Facts

Programming

The ability to program new functions for robots makes them incredibly versatile machines. Programming was pioneered by Joseph Marie Jacquard, who in 1801 developed a way to program automated looms using holes punched in cards.

Integrated Circuits

Integrated circuits, which combine the functions of several different computer parts onto one tiny chip, made it possible to build smaller, cheaper, faster computing devices. This development drove the creation of more efficient robots.

Robotic Arms

Robots entered widespread use after the development of the robotic arm, which could easily be integrated into assembly lines at factories. The later invention of the Direct Drive Robotic Arm made robotic arms more precise and reliable.

IMPACT ON SCIENCE

The desire to create better robots has led to research in a vast array of fields, ranging from computer processing to artificial intelligence to mechanical engineering. Medical robots have made precise surgery possible. Remotely controlled robots have made incredible scientific discoveries in deep space and on the ocean floor.

IMPACT ON CULTURE

The term *robot* came from the world of popular culture rather than science, and the field of robotics has continued to have a close relationship with culture. Science-fiction books and movies have long featured robots as characters. Primitive automatons and robots have been used to impress crowds at exhibitions and demonstrations for centuries. More recently, domestic robots have entered our daily lives. Millions of people have their floors vacuumed by robots. Military robots have sparked moral and ethical discussions about whether robots should have the power to kill people autonomously. Today, many of the issues posed by early science-fiction writers about robots have become reality.

QUOTE

"If every tool, when ordered, or even of its own accord, could do the work that befits it . . . then there would be no need either of apprentices for the master workers or of slaves for the lords."

—*Aristotle*

Glossary

actuator

A motor that moves or controls mechanical systems.

android

A robot built to look like a human.

artificial intelligence

A field of computer science that focuses on building intelligent machines.

automaton

A device capable of reproducing a preset sequence of movements under its own power.

autonomously

Independently.

drone

An aerial vehicle without a human crew.

humanoid

Having human characteristics.

integrated circuit

A group of tiny transistors installed on a small silicon wafer.

manipulator

Another term for a robotic arm.

meltdown

A disaster occurring in a nuclear power plant when fuel overheats and melts through the inner workings of the plant.

orthopaedic

Having to do with muscles and bones.

orthotics

Artificial supports for the limbs or spine.

patent

An exclusive right to produce and sell a particular invention.

prototype

The first sample model of a new design.

robotics

The science that focuses on the research and development of robots.

telepresence

Using video, audio, and robotic technology to be virtually present in a second location.

telerobotic

Controlled remotely by a human.

transistor

An electronic device that controls the flow of electricity.

Additional Resources

Selected Bibliography

Ichbiah, Daniel. *Robots: From Science Fiction to Technological Revolution*. New York: Abrams, 2005. Print.

Wise, Edwin. *Robotics Demystified*. New York: McGraw-Hill, 2005. Print.

Further Readings

Bridgman, Roger. *DK Eyewitness Books: Robot*. New York: DK, 2004. Print.

Jones, David. *Mighty Robots: Mechanical Marvels that Fascinate and Frighten*. Toronto, ON: Annick, 2005. Print.

Websites

To learn more about History of Science, visit **booklinks.abdopublishing.com**. These links are routinely monitored and updated to provide the most current information available.

Artificial Intelligence Center
SRI International
333 Ravenswood Avenue
Menlo Park, CA 94025
650-859-2641

http://www.ai.sri.com

Since the 1960s, the Artificial Intelligence Center has been a key leader in robotics and artificial intelligence research. Once a part of Stanford University, it became independent in 1970 and continues to carry out work as a nonprofit organization.

The Robotics Institute
Carnegie Mellon
5000 Forbes Avenue
Pittsburgh, PA 15213
412-268-3818

http://www.ri.cmu.edu/index.html

The Robotics Institute was the first dedicated robotics department at a university in the United States. Today, it continues to carry out advanced robotics research while training the next generation of robot scientists.

Source Notes

Chapter 1. Robot Responders

1. John D. Sutter. "How 9/11 Inspired a New Era of Robotics." *CNN Tech*. CNN, 7 Sept. 2011. Web. 4 May 2014.

2. Michael Behar. "The New Mobile Infantry." *Wired*. Wired, May 2002. Web. 2 Sept. 2014.

3. Tim Dirks. "Robots in Film: A Complete Illustrated History of Robots in the Movies." *AMC Filmsite*. AMC, 2014. Web. 22 Sept. 2014.

Chapter 2. Early Automatons

None.

Chapter 3. Robots of the Early 1900s

1. Ed Reis. "Early Westinghouse Robots Were Fascinating Characters." *Pittsburgh Engineer*. Engineers' Society of Western Pennsylvania, 2005. Web. 22 Sept. 2014.

2. Ibid.

3. Ibid.

4. "Inside the Lab—Remote Control." *Tesla*. PBS, n.d. Web. 22 Sept. 2014.

5. Arthur Ed LeBouthillier. "W. Grey Walter and His Turtle Robots." *Robotics Society of Southern California*. Robotics Society of Southern California, 2014. Web. 22 Sept. 2014.

Chapter 4. The Birth of Modern Robots

1. "Shakey." *Artificial Intelligence Center*. SRI International, 2014. Web. 22 Sept. 2014.

2. K. Jarayajan and Manjit Singh. "Master-Slave Manipulators: Technology and Recent Developments." *BARC Newsletter*. BARC, June 2006. Web. 22 Sept. 2014.

3. Doris Kilbane. "Joseph Engelberger: Robotics Move From Industry to Space to Elder Care." *Electronic Design*. Electronic Design, 1 Dec. 2008. Web. 22 Sept. 2014.

4. "About RI." *The Robotics Institute*. Carnegie Mellon, n.d. Web. 22 Sept. 2014.

5. "1958: Integrated Circuit Invented by Jack Kilby." *Timeline*. Texas Instruments, 2008. Web. 22 Sept. 2014.

6. Saswato R. Das. "The Chip That Changed the World." *New York Times*. New York Times, 19 Sept. 2008. Web. 22 Sept. 2014.

Chapter 5. Industrial Robots

1. George ElKoura and Karan Singh. "Handrix: Animating the Human Hand." *SIGGRAPH Symposium on Computer Animation*. Eurographics, 2003. Web. 22 Sept. 2014.

2. Michael E. Moran. "Evolution of Robotic Arms." *Journal of Robotic Surgery* 1.2 (July 2007): 103–111. Web. 22 Sept. 2014.

3. "World Robotics 2013 Industrial Robots." *International Federation of Robotics*. International Federation of Robotics, n.d. Web. 22 Sept. 2014.

4. "History." *International Federation of Robotics*. International Federation of Robotics, n.d. Web. 22 Sept. 2014.

5. Gordon Orr. "Coming to a Factory Near You: Chinese Robots." *Gordon's View*. McKinsey & Company Greater China, 10 Apr. 2014. Web. 22 Sept. 2014.

$$\frac{a+b}{a} = \frac{a}{b} = 1.618$$

Source Notes Continued

Chapter 6. Research and Service Robots

1. "Explorer 1 Overview." *NASA*. NASA, 30 Jan. 2008. Web. 22 Sept. 2014.

2. "Hubble Essentials: Quick Facts." *The Telescope*. HubbleSite.org, n.d. Web. 22 Sept. 2014.

3. "The Development of a Legend." *Historic First Moves*. Canadian Space Agency, 7 Nov. 2011. Web. 22 Sept. 2014.

4. "Space Travel Enters the 15th Century." *BBC News*. BBC, 13 Aug. 1998. Web. 22 Sept. 2014.

5. "From Submarines to Robots: Exploring the Deep Ocean." *Ocean Portal*. Smithsonian National Museum of Natural History, n.d. Web. 22 Sept. 2014.

6. Sandra Blakeslee. "A Robot Arm Assists in 3 Brain Operations." *New York Times*. New York Times, 25 June 1985. Web. 22 Sept. 2014.

7. "Who We Are." *Ekso Bionics*. Ekso Bionics, 2013. Web. 22 Sept. 2014.

8. "Our History." *iRobot*. iRobot, 2013. Web. 22 Sept. 2014.

9. Daniel Ichbiah. *Robots: From Science Fiction to Technological Revolution*. New York: Abrams, 2005. Print. 397.

10. Eddie Wrenn. "He's Back! Furby—the Christmas Craze of 1998—Returns in a Bid to Be 2012's Must-Have Present." *Daily Mail*. Daily Mail, 15 May 2012. Web. 22 Sept. 2014.

Chapter 7. Rescue and War Robots

1. P. W. Singer. "Military Robots and the Laws of War." *The New Atlantis*. The New Atlantis, 2009. Web. 22 Sept. 2014.

2. Elisabeth Bumiller and Thom Shanker. "War Evolves with Drones, Some Tiny as Bugs." *New York Times*. New York Times, 19 June 2011. Web. 22 Sept. 2014.

3. Ibid.

4. "Portable Ground Station." *UAV Factory*. UAV Factory, n.d. Web. 22 Sept. 2014.

5. "Hermes 900." *Elbit Systems*. Elbit Systems, 2014. Web. 22 Sept. 2014.

6. P. W. Singer. "Military Robots and the Laws of War." *The New Atlantis*. The New Atlantis, 2009. Web. 22 Sept. 2014.

7. P. W. Singer. "Drones Don't Die: A History of Military Robotics." *Military History Magazine*. HistoryNet.com, 5 May 2011. Web. 22 Sept. 2014.

8. Daniel Ichbiah. *Robots: From Science Fiction to Technological Revolution*. New York: Abrams, 2005. Print. 332.

9. "Unmanned Vehicles for US Naval Forces: Background and Issues for Congress." *The Navy Department Library*. US Navy, 25 Oct. 2006. Web. 22 Sept. 2014.

10. Antoine Martin. "US Expands Use of Underwater Unmanned Vehicles." *National Defense*. National Defense, Apr. 2012. Web. 22 Sept. 2014.

11. Douglas Main. "Robots to the Rescue." *Popular Science*. Popular Science, 8 Apr. 2013. Web. 22 Sept. 2014.

12. "Throwbot XT with Audio Capabilities." *Recon Robotics*. Recon Robotics, 2014. Web. 22 Sept. 2014.

13. Christopher Anderson. "Soviet Official Admits That Robots Couldn't Handle Chernobyl Cleanup." *The Scientist*. LabX Media Group, 20 Jan. 1990. Web. 22 Sept. 2014.

14. Marc Raibert, Kevin Blankespoor, Gabriel Nelson, and Rob Playter. "BigDog, the Rough-Terrain Quadruped Robot." *Boston Dynamics*. Boston Dynamics, 8 Apr. 2008. Web. 22 Sept. 2014.

Chapter 8. The Future of Robotics

1. Carl Haub. "World Population Aging: Clocks Illustrate Growth in Population Under Age 5 and Over Age 65." *Population Reference Bureau*. PRB, Jan. 2011. Web. 22 Sept. 2014.

2. "Latest Robot Can Pick Strawberry Fields Forever." *Japan Times*. Japan Times, 26 Sept. 2013. Web. 22 Sept. 2014.

3. Adam Clark Estes. "Meet Google's Robot Army. It's Growing." *Gizmodo*. Gizmodo, 27 Jan. 2014. Web. 22 Sept. 2014.

4. Tim Hornyak. "Meet Pepper, the 'Love-Powered' Humanoid Robot That Knows How You're Feeling." *PC World*. PC World, 5 June 2014. Web. 22 Sept. 2014.

5. Ibid.

6. "UN Meeting Targets 'Killer Robots.'" *UN News Center*. United Nations, 14 May 2014. Web. 22 Sept. 2014.

7. "Positive Impact of Industrial Robots on Employment." *International Federation of Robotics*. International Federation of Robotics, 21 Feb. 2011. Web. 22 Sept. 2014.

Index

About the Author

Racquel Foran is a freelance writer who lives in British Columbia, Canada. In addition to having written a number of juvenile reference books on topics as varied as developing nations' debt, North Korea, and organ transplants, Foran also publishes a dance magazine that targets young readers. She is dedicated to fostering a love of reading and learning in children.